Mum ♡
2017

Doreen Hinchliffe

Dark Italics

Indigo Dreams Publishing

First Edition: Dark Italics
First published in Great Britain in 2017 by:
Indigo Dreams Publishing
24, Forest Houses
Cookworthy Moor
Halwill
Beaworthy
Devon
EX21 5UU

www.indigodreams.co.uk

Doreen Hinchliffe has asserted her right under the Copyright,
Designs and Patents Act 1988 to be identified as the author of
this work.
© Doreen Hinchliffe 2017

ISBN 978-1-910834-58-9
British Library Cataloguing in Publication Data. A CIP record
for this book can be obtained from the British Library.

Designed and typeset in Palatino Linotype by Indigo Dreams.
Cover design Ronnie Goodyer at Indigo Dreams
Printed and bound in Great Britain by 4edge Ltd.

Papers used by Indigo Dreams are recyclable products made
from wood grown in sustainable forests following the guidance
of the Forest Stewardship Council.

In loving memory
of my parents and grandparents

Acknowledgements

I would like to thank the following people for their help in the compilation of this collection:
Tamar Yoseloff for her invaluable advice, support and encouragement; the members of Greenwich Poetry Workshop for their constructive suggestions on a number of the poems; Lin Jonas for her assistance with proof-reading.

Some of these poems, or versions of them, have appeared in Acumen, Artemis, CPR International, Dream Catcher, Equinox, Magma, Mslexia, Orbis, South, Obsessed With Pipework, The Interpreter's House, Weyfarers and Writers' Forum and have won prizes or commendations in the Live Canon Poetry Competition, London Writers' Competition, Northampton Literature Group Competition, Ottaker and Faber's Poetry Competition, Peterloo Poetry Competition, Petra Kenney Poetry Competition (twice), The Plough Poetry Prize, Torriano Poetry Competition and Ware Poetry Competition.

Dark Italics is Doreen Hinchliffe's debut collection.

CONTENTS

The Questions Mirrors Ask 9

In Fading Light 10

Café Picasso 11

Triangle 12

End Of The Affair 13

My Last Husband 14

The Newlyweds 16

Reflection 17

Intermezzo 18

The Resident 19

How We Were Before 20

Visiting Time 21

Elegy 22

History Lesson 23

Miltiades At Marathon 24

King Wladyslaw's Lament 25

Machiavelli Struts His Stuff 26

All Their Yesterdays 27

Pierrot 29

A Moment In The Sun 30

Time Travelling 32

War Dead, The Devonshire Cemetery, Mametz 33

Buckfastleigh 34

The Violinist 36

After Such Knowledge 37

Making Sense Of The Event 38

What Survives Of Us 39

Hand On Heart 40

Passing Over 42

Opening Time

Opening Time 43

Jack The Barman 46

The Hawk 47

The Magic Touch 48

Tap Room Ted 50

Guinness Lizzie 51

Alfred Tunnicliffe 52

Nowt Nor Summat 54

Catchphrase Charlie 55

Alice and Norman 56

Norman Wisdom 57

Charlie Chaplin 58

Helena Rubenstein 59

Coaly 60

Pat and Roland 61

Rag and Bone 62

Bomber Harris 63

Mrs. Malaprop 64

Peggy and Hedley 65

The Regular 66

Closing Time: Christmas 1965 68

Dark Italics

The Questions Mirrors Ask

The questions mirrors ask persist,
throbbing their relentless bass.
Who is this 'you'? Does 'you' exist?

A child breathes on the glass and mist
obscures the outline of his face.
The questions mirrors ask persist.

Reflections haunt and probe, insist
that what is not could be the case.
Who is this 'you'? Does 'you' exist?

We stare, unable to resist
the way the glass marks time in space.
The questions mirrors ask persist.

Each looking-glass turns terrorist
and threatens to usurp our place.
Who is this 'you'? Does 'you' exist?

The mirror hides a final twist.
Held to our lips, it leaves no trace.
The questions mirrors ask persist.
Are you still here? Do you exist?

In Fading Light

She works beneath the window in the pause
between dusk and dark, embroidery frame
upon her lap, needle unpicking flaws

in a tapestry that bears her name.
Hope is rare and fleeting now, leaves
a mark as faint as the flecks of sun that came

to her at dawn, flickering on her sleeves.
Happiness no longer lasts for days,
no longer folds itself around her or weaves

across the fabric of her soul in a blaze
of gold. She knows more sombre tones: the deep
browns of Rembrandt, the misty blues and greys

of Whistler. They would want to paint her, keep
the way the light catches her face, the white
in her hair and how she'll be too proud to weep

when all her colours fade into the night.

Café Picasso

The air is heavy, thick,
redolent of smoke from cigarettes
that down the years
has wreathed its way
through rainy afternoons.
They sit alone, as usual,
killing time beneath a dingy light,
Harlequin and Columbine,
eking out their wine until
the clowns arrive
to mark the interval.

Both stare into the distance,
gaze beyond the smoke.
She's thinking of a ringmaster –
how she curled his hair
around her little finger,
sure that love would last.
He's thinking of sawdust –
tiny shavings
clinging between the toes
of the fire-eater's daughter,
who amused him for a while.

They did talk once, long since,
their kindred spirits courted
danger on the high trapeze,
but that was when the animals were wild,
before it all became just horses,
jugglers, acrobats, parades.
Now, they walk in tame procession
in costumes that have faded –
their safety net no longer needed.

Triangle

I don't imagine you intended harm
or even understand the life I miss,
or what you hold so lightly in your palm.

I've often thought about the way you kiss,
since that October night I found your note;
the crumpled page that told of mutual bliss

had rustled in the lining of his coat.
I watch myself smooth out each crease and read
and run my finger over what you wrote.

I don't suppose you know how much I need,
desire him still, that even though our days
have turned to grey, the past will not recede.

Like you, I love his faults and crave his praise.
We talk just as we did before he lied,
although he never quite returns my gaze.

A thousand times I've questioned why you hide
and why he never leaves me for your sake,
but time has told me we are held inside

a triangle of fear that none dare break,
against whose grip we know there's no defence –
for each of us there's far too much at stake.

Some days I wonder if you ever sense,
like me, the presence of a ghostly third.
In dreams we meet; our silence is immense.

It mocks the futile tread of every word.

End Of The Affair

Like a film that flickers in my head
the scene replays itself as dawn is breaking,
in that blurred crossing between sleep and waking
when darkness speaks the language of the dead.

I'm driving over moors. The moon is new.
Its crescent cuts through cloud, but casts no shadow
and, like some winding thought I fear to follow,
the road is leading me away from you.

As usual, we'd talked for hours that night
trying to salvage what we knew was lost,
circling the remnants of our secret past.
As I left, the world was turning white,

back gardens shivered in the freezing air.
I crept outside, still wary of the neighbours,
but biting cold closed curtains, silenced rumours
and carved in ice the end of the affair,

except, through half-closed eyes, I see you still,
your anxious face receding, pale as death,
behind the smoke-rings of your frosted breath
forever waving, mouthing your farewell.

My Last Husband

That's my last husband hanging on the wall,
looking as if he ruled the roost. He's tall
and very handsome, don't you think? His hair's
not straight but then I caught him unawares.
He hadn't put his Brylcreem on, you know,
that's why, perhaps, his bald patch tends to show.
He never liked this photo. Made him look
too old, he said. I found it in a book
after he died and put it up. I bought
the frame myself. 'He can't complain,' I thought,
though, once, he was well practised in the art.
Don't get me wrong, he had a loving heart
as all the ladies in the district knew,
especially the pretty ones, like you.

What's that you say? You never saw me grieve?
But I don't wear my heart upon my sleeve,
my dear. Please, don't weep. He's passed away.
I don't believe there's any more to say.
No, no pain. He didn't suffer long.
In fact, considering he was very strong,
he died quite easily. He'd just gone round
the back with his beloved Basset hound
and there, in the gathering gloom, the hand of fate
dealt him a quick and heavy blow. A slate
it was that felled him, from the roof they say.
I wasn't with him. No, not far away.
The attic, dear. Oh yes, I saw it fall
but, sadly, didn't have the wherewithal
to warn him or cry out. I ran down fast
of course, but he'd already breathed his last.
No, since his death, I've slept, dear, like a log,
knowing he's safely buried, with his dog.

Enough of him, let's go downstairs and eat,
I think that you deserve a little treat.
I know you're fond of cognac, I am too,
and so I've made this specially for you –
a dark and potent brandy-based liqueur
the first of many such delights, I'm sure . . .

The Newlyweds

I think about you often, how just hours after
wedding bells and holy vows, you drowned in shallow waters.
Did you make a pact to paddle there, enticed by thoughts
of scrambling in secret on wet rocks while waiters

were busy serving wine to guests at your reception?
Were you drunk on pink champagne, as one report implies,
or like excited children, unaware of danger, daring
each other to leap from bank to bank in three great strides?

If you had only waited, chatted to the locals,
maybe they'd have warned you to be wary of the current,
told you how, with nearby Bolton Abbey heavy with cloud,
the river gathers force and quickly turns to torrent?

I doubt it. I'm sure they would have known that newlyweds
and cautionary tales don't mix. Wishing you happiness,
they'd have waved you off, watched you striding hand in hand
towards your death in morning suit and bridal dress.

I'm haunted by the question of what happened next.
Was it the swirling force of sudden flood that pulled you under
or a lovers' tiff, a teasing push, that tipped you in,
the weight of wedding clothes causing you to flounder

in the icy flow? Did you slip, then tumble
both at once, or did one of you fall first perhaps,
the other bravely risking everything to help? I think
of how they found you three days later, hands still clasped

and wedding rings intact. Were your final moments
snatched by fear and rising panic as you guessed that this
must be the end, or, as you clung together swallowing water,
was there time and space enough for one last kiss?

Reflection

The pool bids me linger, perhaps forever.
Lured by its endless peace, its promises,
I gaze deeper into the heart of water.
It wavers, trembling like a distant echo.
My reflection haunts, restores forgotten beauty
fresh as mountain snows on high Olympus.
Icy ripples trickle through my fingers.
Eager to cup my hands, slake my thirst,
I force my limbs to kneel and lower my lips.
No leaf or twig floats on the virgin meniscus
although it lies in the shade of oak and cypress.
A welcome refuge from the heat of day,
the water is an oasis, dark, inviting . . .

The water is an oasis, dark, inviting,
a welcome refuge from the heat of day.
Although it lies in the shade of oak and cypress,
no leaf or twig floats on the virgin meniscus.
I force my limbs to kneel and lower my lips,
eager to cup my hands, slake my thirst.
Icy ripples trickle through my fingers,
fresh as mountain snows on high Olympus.
My reflection haunts, restores forgotten beauty.
It wavers, trembling like a distant echo.
I gaze deeper into the heart of water,
lured by its endless peace, its promises.
The pool bids me linger, perhaps forever.

Intermezzo

One a.m. In bed, but wide awake,
I'm trapped in a prolonged commercial break.
Intermission popcorn in my throat
I press the menopause on my remote
control, take stock, and pose a host of wild
questions, bigger than those I asked as a child.
Are my symptoms real or in my mind?
Do I want fast forward or rewind?
Am I going through a mid-life crisis?
Is this stiffness in my joints arthritis?
Should I take up jogging or aerobics?
Start a self-help group for ageing phobics?
Am I moody, broody or plain mad?
Clinically depressed or only sad?
Should I ask a toy boy for a date?
Dare I make that phone call to RELATE?

Oblivious, you stretch your legs and sigh.
In twenty years you've never wondered why
I've seemed detached, withdrawn, nor do you now.
Your arm around my waist, you tell me how
the way I feel is really nothing strange,
then joke it's what your mother called *the change*.
You turn away, return to sleep, leaving
a thousand more unanswered questions breathing
beside the poems of Stevie Smith under
my bedside lamp. I look at you and wonder,
can I find some way in time remaining
to tell you I'm not waxing, dear, but waning?

The Resident

I'll never now race bareback in the snow
or probe the ancient mysteries of caves,
never glide the heavens or ride the waves
or plant my flag on peaks where none dare go.
I'll never watch a salmon leap the falls
or plumb the ocean's hidden blues and greens
except, perhaps, vicariously, through screens
or third rate art on institution walls.
My shrunken world is framed by leaded lights
and sliding patio doors and frosted glass,
its hours told by cups of tea and meals.
Yet, sometimes, on warm lingering summer nights,
I catch the smell of pine leaves, new mown grass,
faint remnants clinging round a trolley's wheels.

How We Were Before

Don't you remember how we were before
your brightness yielded slowly to the night?
Have you forgotten only words or more?

You'd leave at six and gently close the door.
We'd always kiss in early morning light.
Don't you remember how we were before?

You played with Ruth when you came home at four,
taught her to ride her bike, to fly her kite.
Have you forgotten only words or more?

You used to go for runs along the shore.
I'd shout and wave till you were out of sight.
Don't you remember how we were before?

My shell shocked veteran from a private war,
you stand aloof somewhere remote and white.
Have you forgotten only words or more?

Come down, lie here beside me on the floor;
come back to me just once and hold me tight.
Don't you remember how we were before?
Have you forgotten only words or more?

Visiting Time

I didn't wear a gown
the hour you arrived,
though life gushed red on the forceps
staining me with crimson drops.
I watched, wide-eyed, transfixed,
the strange sticky business of birth
and how your nails shone in the light
like the ivory on my piano.
They wrapped you in a white shawl
and folded it over twice.

I didn't wear a coat
the night you cried,
though water welled on the doorstep
drowning my floundering key in the lock.
I watched myself return to
the unfinished business of Christmas – half-eaten
chocolates, the wax on burnt-out candles
like tiny icicle fingers –
then scribbled the milkman a white note
and folded it over twice.

I didn't wear a hat
the day you died,
though summer scorched my forehead
searing the charred remains of my mind.
I watched in disbelief
the bleak brisk business of departure
and shadows strewn around the sunset
like the toys of a sleeping child.
They wrapped you in a white sheet
and folded it over twice.

Elegy

Stripped bare of blossom by late April hail,
your cherry tree stands naked in the park,
lit by a watery sun that smears a trail
of pallid gold across its ancient bark.
Inside our room, a single washed-out ray
uncovers dust around the barley twist
of your old chair. I brush it all away,
the dust you used to say I always missed.
Now, you are missed and what remains of you
remains beyond my reach, no matter how
I might imagine you in sunlight through
the window or beneath the cherry bough.
Our past, like blossom, can't survive the storm;
the sun is powerless to keep it warm.

History Lesson

I trace the slant of rays through windows and on walls.
Every voice is silent now, the classroom hushed;
on my shoulders history, like sunlight, falls,
floating on tiny particles of chalky dust.

Every voice is silent now, the classroom hushed.
Ink is trickling back to ink wells, staining floors.
Floating on tiny particles of chalky dust
the distant murmurs drift down empty corridors.

Ink is trickling back to ink wells, staining floors;
time has smudged the past and present into one.
The distant murmurs drift down empty corridors.
I feel the gentle tug and nudge of lives long gone.

Time has smudged the past and present into one.
I catch the furtive giggles, whispers behind hands.
I feel the gentle tug and nudge of lives long gone,
those who spun the globe and dreamed of foreign lands.

I catch the furtive giggles, whispers behind hands.
Inside the desks I glimpse the crumpled notes they hid,
those who spun the globe and dreamed of foreign lands.
I read their bored initials etched on every lid.

Inside the desks I glimpse the crumpled notes they hid.
I trace the slant of rays through windows and on walls.
I read their bored initials etched on every lid.
On my shoulders, history, like sunlight, falls.

Miltiades At Marathon

Dawn. I wait for the blood-red rim of the sun
to bronze the barren hills, burnish our spears.
The men fall silent, each one facing fears
he dare not voice. Outnumbered three to one,
we hesitate. I seize our only chance,
insist we swell the ranks to left and right.
Ten thousand helmets blind me with their light.
The fate of Athens turns on this advance.
I give the sign. We cross the plain with ease,
attack, encircle them, our mad endeavour
crowned with victory. It feels so sweet,
and yet, somehow, so final. Pheidippides,
my younger self, goes running through the heat.
I watch him disappear, as if forever.

Miltiades was the Greek general who led his men into battle at Marathon. His strategy of having more men on the flanks enabled the Greeks to surround the Persians and win a famous victory. However, it proved to be his last success. Barely one year later, when he failed in an expedition against the island of Paros, he was cast into prison, where he subsequently died.

Pheidippides ran the 26 miles back to Athens in order to announce the victory and died of a heart attack as he breathed the word 'nike'.

King Wladyslaw's Lament

The sun went round the earth when he began
to shift the view, unfix the globe. I wait
in semi-darkness, beside his pencilled plan
of heavenly bodies, his astrolabe and great
wooden compass, listening for the chime
of a clock. I, too, yearn to change the scene
but I'm enslaved, a prisoner of the time;
my view is fixed, I stand behind the queen.
Twice a day we judder through the door,
process to bells and camera clicks, the *oohs*
and *aahs* of tourists. All these I now ignore.
I seek to capture what I'm doomed to lose –
a hint of amethyst beneath the eaves
and sunlight filtered through a sieve of leaves.

*King Wladyslaw is one of six wooden figures that process around the
Collegium Maius clock in the courtyard of Krakow's oldest university. When
at rest behind the clock, these figures, all associated with the college's history,
occupy part of the room where Nikolas Copernicus studied in the 1490s.*

Machiavelli Struts His Stuff

My habits are nocturnal. I conceal
my form, seek darkness, lurk in shadow, skulk
round every corner, reluctant to reveal
myself in honest light of day. My bulk

is heavy with the weight of subterfuge.
Crammed full of all the lies on which I feed,
my brain's capacity has swelled to huge
proportions. I thrive upon connivance, breed

hypocrisy, I'll con you every time.
I curry favours, promise to deliver
and then don't. My element is slime,
through which I crawl or worm my way or slither.

I'm underhand. I take you in then preen
when you have gone. I bask in my self-praise,
inhabiting a world that, being green,
is easy prey to disingenuous ways.

I'll scheme in any currency. My stacks
of notes are all crisp counterfeit, so each
transaction made below the counter smacks
of double-dealing. I never overreach

myself. In fact, my artistry complete,
I rest assured posterity will make
my name a synonym of cool deceit.
I'm the genuine article – a fake.

All Their Yesterdays

Macbeth:
Now we're all their yesterdays my friend,
their 'A' levels are finally at an end
and once again our words have lighted fools
the way to dusty exit doors in schools.
We're gone, forgotten, locked away in drawers;
they think they've mastered all our fatal flaws.
We're only useful for a while, dear Ham;
they pinch all our best lines for their exam
and then, like Lady M, they wash their hands
of us. We disappear from all their plans.
They just abandon us without contrition.
I wish they weren't so lacking in ambition!

Hamlet:
You could be right Macbeth, need I say more;
it isn't in my nature to be sure.
I should have waited, should have thought a fraction
longer about thinking about action.
Perhaps if I'd procrastinated further,
then you and I might have been spared this *murther*
that happens every year in English schools
and turns us into set books, lists of rules.
It's all too much! It really isn't fair
to multiply those shocks to which I'm heir.
To be is butchered yearly by 2B
and now I'm simplified for key stage three!
Just like Ophelia, I've been watered down;
they're even saying that I *made* her drown.
Polonius's death is just a farce –
they all pronounce his *arras* as his *arse*.
Once, they praised my intellect's refinements
but since those damned continuous assignments,

no one can do me justice any more.
I'm thought of as a wimp who'll never score
with women. It isn't cool, it isn't done
to tell your girl friend to become a nun.
You're out of kilter Mac, I'm prehistoric.
To them, we're both of us (alas) poor Yorick!

Pierrot

(after 'A Dressing-Room For Gilles' by Joseph Cornell)

I'm stuck in this hall of mirrors
haunted by reflections of a self
that you created down the ages.
Defined by my clothes, I was a
puppet fashioned to your liking
a pantomime clown. No longer
twinned with Columbine, I am
abandoned and alone, my head

cleanly sundered from its trunk
my hands dangling from baggy
sleeves that match the pallor of
my powdered face and pointed
hat. Six pom-poms weave dark
magic down my chest. Delicate
silks balloon around my narrow
hips, accentuate the space now
fixed between my body and my

freshly amputated legs. Draped
in pantaloons, they jerk in time
to lost songs, belie the seeming
comfort of slippered feet. Why
have you spliced me into three
turned me into a jigsaw for the
disgruntled child, boxed me up
in this dressing-room, its walls
lined with the hateful prints of
harlequin, its glass etched with
his diamonds, its panels coated
with his rainbow-coloured cuts.

A Moment In The Sun

(Daguerre's 'Boulevard Du Temple' (1838) is the first
photograph in which people are visible)

A shorter exposure time and I'd have been there,
dancing between the shoe-shine boy
and the old man on the bench

or skipping past the house on the corner
with the child peeping round a curtain,
the woman at an upstairs window.

Like them, I could have lived forever,
my slender figure immortalised
and gazed on far into the future,

its outline shadowy, but there,
captured on a sheet of silver-plated copper
and preserved beneath this pane of glass.

My one mistake was moving.
Only perfect stillness, sustained for minutes,
etched itself on the fragile surface.

That's why, like all the bustle of the street,
the clattering carts and cabs, the carriages,
the rumbling horse-drawn omnibus

and all the ladies strolling down
the boulevard with fluttering parasols,
I disappeared. Look. No trace of me remains.

A few more years, perhaps,
a different camera, larger faster lens
and I might have been a blur, a ghost,

still faint, but clearly visible, the sun
warming my hair as I leap to touch
a leaf on the stooping sycamore.

Time Travelling

They stare at me, this couple I don't know,
posing by potted palms and an array
of flowers. Framed in sepia, they show
their reverence for the camera by the way
they stand – upright, proud, their faces stern,
unsmiling. A gravitas surrounds them, a sure
sense that through this moment they will earn
their place in history, make time secure.
He chose to wear his Sunday suit; she chose
her best white blouse, its collar trimmed with lace.
Her eyes are just like grandma's; his upturned nose
just like my mother's. There's no obvious trace
of me and yet I'm theirs and they are mine.
Our fingers touch. It's 1889.

War Dead, The Devonshire Cemetery, Mametz

They lie no more in blood-filled trenches,
free, now, to dream of hawthorn hedges
or moonlight falling on the black-tipped tails of foxes.

They hear again the old, familiar noises,
not of guns, but home – the chitter of finches,
the ringing of bells, the slow clip-clop of horses.

Their smooth white bones, fragile as lilies,
recall young boys with newly-whiskered faces,
embarrassed by their mothers' farewell kisses.

Tucked beneath the rows of stones and crosses,
they're meant to sing of duty, sacrifices,
courage in battle and how short life is.

They don't. They can't. Their canticles
are only of the sun, the manacles
of war long gone. They've slipped their shackles.

Buckfastleigh

Steam rises hot in his nostrils. The train
snorts, coughing smoke. He hugs his case,
fingers the label on his gabardine,
presses his face to the grime of carriage glass

and peers across the platform through a fog
that shrouds a mass of faces, anxious, sad.
His mother's hanky flutters like a flag
above the crowds. She mouths to him, *Be good!*

The train sighs heavily, heaves its weight
forward, straining to reach the first bend.
Her handkerchief slowly fades to a blur of white,
surrenders him to distant, alien land.

He curls up in his seat, feels the brush
of moquette against the side of his leg, his jaw.
Forehead pressed to the window, he thinks of the fish
he won at the fair, his frogspawn in a jar.

The engine's rhythm lulls as they leave the town.
He stares, unseeing, at endless lines of wire
on telegraph poles and steep embankments strewn
with poppies from an older, different war.

They chug through yellow fields, past sheep and cows
and scarecrows like the ones in picture books.
It's almost five when the engine finally slows,
easing to a halt with a hiss of brakes.

Strangers line the platform, holding up names
of children to be sheltered from invasion.
The air feels far too clean, devoid of fumes.
He waits his turn, then steps out on the station,

its name inscribed on the sign he walks towards
in perfect, stark italics – *Buckfastleigh*.
He thinks of home, his father's parting words.
Don't cry, big boys don't cry, he whispers softly.

The Violinist

I played the violin to stay alive
while thousands turned to ashes in the fire.
It was the only way I could survive.

Pretending that such music might revive
our souls, rekindle hope, desire,
I played the violin to stay alive.

I heard the rattle of each train arrive
but focussed only on the grey barbed wire.
It was the only way I could survive.

With marches and mazurkas I would drive
out screams that rose up like a keening choir.
I played the violin to stay alive.

I was simply B6945,
immune to smells of dead flesh in the mire.
It was the only way I could survive.

This is the honest truth, yet still I strive
to suffocate a voice that calls me liar.
I played the violin to stay alive.
It was the only way I could survive.

After Such Knowledge

'After such knowledge, what forgiveness?' 'Gerontion' by T.S. Eliot

'I crammed them onto every train,
then closed the doors to stop them flooding back.'

'I saw them steam across the plain
and worked the points that sent them down the track.'

'I counted them when they came in,
divided young from old and weak from strong.'

'I stained the number on their skin
and broke the bones of those who took too long.'

'I marched them briskly to their fate
and silenced them with beatings and with threats.'

'I stripped them naked at the gate
and rifled through their clothes for cigarettes.'

'I supervised the showering,
released the gas then sealed the hatches tight.'

'We never did a single thing,
just watched them shuffle off into the night.'

Making Sense Of The Event

In oppressive noontide heat we chanted
names of distant battles, the where and when
of British conquests. Relentless sunlight slanted
through high windows and throbbed inside my head,
its drumming loud, insistent. I sensed, back then,
unease, but didn't think this could be said.

All summer I swatted flies, tugged at flowers
for tucked-away bees, dug deep for worms and felt
them squirm, or yanked the legs off spiders. Hours
I spent alone, scouring the dusty lane
for prey, tasted wet salt sometimes, as I knelt
on nettles, but didn't feel that this was pain.

The leaves turned brown. Other kids climbed trees
for conkers. I hid in the wood, knee deep in mud,
air rifle cocked. Easy as shelling peas
it was. The best a blackbird in full song,
my pellet lodged in its throat. I daubed its blood
on my head but didn't know that this was wrong.

A pale yellow sky darkened to black.
Allotments shivered in the freezing air.
I picked the lock, eased the shed door back.
One kick and the cupboard split. The coast was clear.
I seized my prize, watched it tremble there
in my hands but didn't see that this was fear.

Next morning I was woken by a light
that told me it had snowed. The time, I knew,
had come. The school was full, a snowball fight
begun. The thirty-eight was deep inside
my coat. I saw red white and flashing blue
exploding . . . and didn't care who lived or died.

What Survives Of Us

He roams the streets, reliving old campaigns,
an endless stretch of railroad in his head
that winds beyond Dunkirk and monsoon rains
of Burma to boyhood smells of gasworks, soot,
the mysteries of a dried-up river bed,
the chunter of its pebbles underfoot.

He passes bars and restaurant windows where
the candles burn in lovers' eyes, his pace
slowing as early wallflowers scent the air.
The sudden flicker of a street lamp taunts –
gaslight glimmers on her upturned face,
a waltz from a deserted ballroom haunts.

He shuffles on, probes bins for butt-ends, beer
at the bottom of cans. A busker scrapes a tune
and he's back in uniform, a silver sphere
scattering light around her hair and great
uplifted space glistening above. *Blue Moon*
fades as he walks. It's cold and getting late.

The city owns him now, wraps its scraps
around him, offers coins or lets him doze
in doorways thinking him drunk, half-crazed perhaps,
unaware that love has left its trace
of fire, how still, in dreams, he sees her close
the kissing-gate, her dress a cloud of lace.

Hand On Heart

the thickening rim of the sun
glows red on the horizon
daubs crimson on a grey dawn

washing strung from balconies
flaps in the wind
shivers in early morning air

echoes drift down alleyways
rumble of wheels
chatter of women

the winding streets are waking
time to descend
time to unbar the door

I mingle with the crowds
my face like any other
in the marketplace

I have learned to blend in
studied how to linger
how to barter over bruised skins

I scan the rows of fruit
finger a pomegranate
sink my thumb in a black avocado

prepared to watch and wait
for unblemished sweetness
perfect ripeness

jostled by the growing throng
I thrust an elbow out
and slide my palm inside my coat

I feel the harness tighten
locate the detonator switch
and then the die is cast

my oath is sworn
with hand on heart
my hour come round at last

Passing Over

The first passes over. She looks tired.
She hears its engine buzzing overhead,
sees silver wings across a cloudless sky
and long thin trails of vapour far away.
Scanning the horizon, she imagines
reaching borders with no papers and yearns
for a land she used to dream about – her secret,
private country, not on any chart.

The second passes over. She looks up,
shielding her face, hardly daring to hope.
Stranded in searing heat, she has said
nothing for days, too weary to speak, with shade
hard to find and water scarce and her bones
aching from endless trekking over the stony
mountain ridge. The sound of the aircraft's drone
grows fainter, leaving only the throb of the sun.

The third passes over. She looks asleep,
her body resting gently against a slope
shadowed by rocks. A chopper circles way
above her, its blades rotating through the dry,
dusty air. The pilot spots the barren
plateau below and lands, a rescue plan
in place at last. Thousands rise as one.
They surge forward, pleading. She sleeps on.

Opening Time

A sequence of poems reflecting the author's childhood
in the Yorkshire pub run by her parents
and second home to a host of memorable characters

Opening Time

My bed was in an attic room,
sandwiched between a low wall
and stacks of boxes full of glasses
awaiting their eventual call

to the bar downstairs. Half asleep,
I listened to the final refrain
(goodnight, goodnight), the revving of cars
and the distant hoot of the midnight train.

Sometimes, stirring beneath my blanket,
I overheard Noddy and Rupert Bear
engage in whispered conversation
and opened my eyes wide to stare

at the dark, intrigued by the shapes of toys –
hula hoop and pogo stick
shadowy in a corner, the curved
neck of my rocking horse, old Nick,

his black mane barely visible
in the moonlight. Often, I let
my thoughts wander, reciting the names
of all the customers I'd met

or chanting slowly to myself
the different drinks they ordered – Shandy,
Pale Ale, Guinness, Milk Stout, Snowball,
Port and Lemon, Cherry Brandy . . .

Dizzy with their potency
I drifted to sleep, lulled by the chime
of the grandfather clock in the hall below,
counting the hours to opening time.

Jack The Barman

He ducked beneath the counter, late,
one arm in the sleeve of a waiter's coat,
a *souvenir*, so we were told,
of his days at the Hotel Metropole.
Starched white, it had one button,
which he always let me fasten.

Come on, then, do it up, he'd call.
Good practice for when you go to school.
His rugged face was weathered, lined
from years of piecework on the land,
his dark hair thick with Brylcreem, shiny
and sticky to the touch, like honey.

I loved to help him open a bottle.
Together, we clamped its top in the metal
catch on the bar, then held on tight,
his warm hands steadying mine. I'd wait
for the magic of the drop, the thud
in the bin below, his whispered *good*.

Scaling the shelves, I could stand as tall
as him, name all the coins in the till.
He closed his fist round threepenny bits
and made them disappear. Did tricks
with tanners, half crowns, too. *I call it
'sleight of hand',* he chuckled, his pocket

bulging with silver, his immense
palms raised in innocence.
He left between Christmas and New Year,
blowing kisses in the air
and muttering it was *time to move on*.
I never understood why he'd gone.

The Hawk

The man with no hands gave me lessons in drawing,
holding the pen in his teeth. Wide-eyed,
I watched as, nose first, imps and goblins,
elves and leprechauns appeared.

He used to let me touch his stumps.
Rounded like dumplings and smooth as wax,
they were always icy cold to the touch.
Is that how dead men feel? I'd ask.

Drawing helped his days tick by,
he said. That and rides on his trike.
He showed me his cartoons in *The Dalesman*,
told me his penname was *The Hawk*.

We chatted for hours, built houses
from beer mats. Often, without a word,
I'd fetch my red three-wheeler and ride
beside him round the cobbled yard.

I loved the way he braked with his feet
and steered by slotting both his stumps
in scooped-out bits of leather – *my makeshift
handlebars* he called them once.

He knew a lot of poems by heart –
My Shadow, The Jumblies, The Pied Piper.
One day, he wrote a verse about me,
and put it in the local paper.

When I could read, I recited it over
and over behind my bedroom door.
I know a little maid of three.
I beg her pardon –'nearly four'.

The Magic Touch

Mam never took to cooking,
was constantly frustrated
by the vagaries of flour

the way it frosted the floor,
collected in the cracks
of the old wooden table,

blanched the flowers on her pinny
or strayed into the wayward curls
of her home-permed hair,

sometimes even coating
in a fine white dust
the great cast iron range

in which all manner of her dishes
disappeared and disappointed,
lacking the magic touch.

Undaunted, every Friday
she'd close the door to the bar
and hoist me on the dresser,

inviting me to watch
her weekly tussle
with the mysteries of dough.

She always donned
her forage cap to roll the pastry,
still reliving the war.

Run Rabbit Run
she hummed as she trimmed
the overhanging mass

and thumbed it round the plate,
her clumsy prints stamped
on the crust of every soggy pie.

I'd beg to wear her hat,
pretend to be a wounded Tommy
home from the front.

Her eyes wide open in amazement,
she'd whirl me round and round,
singing of bluebirds, nightingales,

the dough from her face shimmying
through my fingers, the spinning air
a blur of firelight and flour.

Tap Room Ted

He came in every lunch time, parched,
his thirst made keener by the furnace he stoked.
Grime clung to him like lichen,
stuck to the bristles on his chin, the grease round his collar.
His eyes were two gigantic plums astride
the wide bridge of his nose
and when he took off his cap, the line of its pressure mark
circled the sweaty remains of his grey hair.

He didn't stay long in the public bar.
The tap room was his element.
He'd plant his boots on the stone floor to light a Woodbine,
then delve inside a pocket for his tarnished box of snuff.
His nostrils flared as he snorted it up.
Once, he even offered some to me –
Come on little lass,'av a sniff o' this.
Go steady, though. It'll mek' thee eyes water!

Every Thursday he taught me to play cribbage
on an old wooden table ringed with beer stains,
his rasping voice as rough as the cracked bark
of his hands ... *fifteen two, fifteen four, fifteen six,*
two for his heels, one for his nob ... a new language,
laced with smells of strong tobacco and mastered
through a blue haze to the rhythmic thud
of dart on board, the steady shuffle of dominoes.

Guinness Lizzie

Prince came first, black border collie,
reeled her in after him on the long line of his lead.

Frail and headscarfed, she suddenly
came in view, arms flailing, flustered.

He tugged her past the snug to the public bar,
slipping his lead to lollop on the hearthrug.

Free of his frolicking, she'd down
a pint of Guinness in less than a minute,

the first of eight or nine before the dreaded
call of closing time at three.

Hunched by the sizzle of the fire, she wallowed
in the luxury of getting slowly sozzled.

Finally, no longer puzzled by the mysteries
of chain and collar, she'd pounce on Prince,

who, seeing her stagger, suddenly lost
all trace of his desire to drag her through the door.

Apart from *Guinness,* the only words
she ever spoke were – *Don't tell Ernest.*

Alfred Tunnicliffe

He lived in a row of tiny
back-to-backs that rose
steeply towards the blackened
viaduct. Weeds pushed up
through cracks in the cobbled street
and nudged their way to his step.

His house was always silent.
No radio sang or chattered.
The wail of distant trains
lulled him to sleep at sundown,
the scratch and scuffle of birds
in the eaves woke him at dawn.

His doorbell was sounded only
by paperboy or milkman,
or sometimes by me, seeking
escape from ticking clocks
on Sunday afternoons
of rain and dog-eared books.

He'd sit me by the fire
and talk of two world wars,
show me old photographs –
his wedding, his greyhound, Lass,
his wife on Blackpool beach,
his son in battle dress.

Once a week, on Friday,
he came in for his pint.
Inching through the door,
he hobbled past the bar
with his gnarled walking-stick
to slump in his favourite chair.

Often, a few old cronies
joined him in the corner,
shared out twenty Woodbines,
relived their days in the sun.
Laughing, he'd wave his hand
towards a time long gone.

I'll soon be six feet under,
he said one late November.
Don't think I'll make next year.
He died the following week.
Apart from me, one Sunday,
no mourners disturbed his peace.

Nowt Nor Summat

Nay, I'm neither nowt nor summat
gran would say, conquering the summit
of the stairs. *I'm nobbut a nuisance*
these days, always spouting nonsense

and both legs shoved into my arse
any road. It'll only get worse.
Afore too long, I shouldn't wonder,
they'll be calling me over yonder.

Wheelchairs were never even an option.
Tha' won't get me in that contraption
(her words when offered one in chapel).
What does 'ter think I am – a cripple?

At bedtime, eyes alight with laughter
she downed her nightly 'shimmy lifter' –
egg flip laced with Johnny Walker,
her guarantee not a sound would wake her.

It's no good being teetotal, now,
on my last legs with a bar below.
She took to drink to forget her cares,
was *fading fast* for fifteen years.

Catchphrase Charlie

It's that man again, he bellowed. *Brace*
yourselves! Turned out nice again today,
so thought I'd just pop in and show my face.

Came here by Shanks' pony he would say,
tossing his cap and half crown on the bar.
Where there's a will, there's bound to be a way.

Can't stop long. Just called for one quick jar.
Have to go and see a man about
a dog. Can't grumble, not this winter. So far,

so good. Heard the latest? They're going out
on strike, them bloody miners. Shot at dawn
they'd all have been in my day. Couldn't shout

their mouths off then. Don't even know you're born
you lot. Who, me? No, I was never off,
never sick. Worked hard night and morn

for more than fifty year. Not even a cough.
Still fit as a fiddle, footloose, fancy free.
On he went, continuing to scoff

at shoddy *now* compared with *used to be.*
Forgetting about the man, the dog, the time,
he reminisced until we closed, at three,

then tottered home, still dreaming of his prime.

Alice and Norman

He always raised his hat and smiled,
ordered a Double Diamond and a pint of mild.
She headed for the table in the corner,
all eighteen stone of her on a tiny buffet
that almost buckled under her weight.
Red-cheeked and cheery, she leaned back to loosen
the belt of a Dannimac that, long ago, refused to button.

There was never any doubt who was the boss.
He turned to her timidly before last orders,
unsure if he could squeeze in one more round.
Time we were off now, Norman. Half past ten.
Giving in without so much as a murmur,
he gently took her arm, doffing his trilby once again.

She got thinner by degrees.
No one noticed at first but soon the pounds rolled off.
Then Alice did a vanishing trick,
swapped herself for a bag of bones
and a face made even whiter by red lipstick.

An anxious Norman whispered
to the barman in another language
full of alien terminology –
lymphoma, chemotherapy.

He bought her Britvic Orange now
and they began to shuffle out
a little earlier each night.

Then, in a spell of wintry weather,
they stopped coming altogether.

Norman Wisdom

His cap was the resemblance. And the way
he asked for bitter in a nasal whine.
In fact, he was tall and glum, didn't say
a lot. Collected stamps and was a mine
of information on the penny black;
knew every breed of dinosaur; how far
each planet was from earth, but lacked the knack
of making conversation in a bar.
Head down, he'd stand alone, wary, on guard,
drumming his fingers on the counter. Once,
he let it slip his schooldays had been hard,
said he was scoffed at, sometimes called a dunce.
He sidestepped life. Avoided ridicule.
Still scared of being taken for a fool.

Charlie Chaplin

Shine for a dime!
That was his refrain,
his entrance and his exit line,
words that called to mind
his wasted youth trawling the States
in search of an emigrant father
and, together with his tash and waddle of a walk,
moulded him into his nickname.

Over a gill of mild
he raised the curtain on another world,
told tales of goldrush, dandies,
suffragettes and silent movies,
made Woodrow Wilson seem more real than Harold.
(He never spoke of the soap he sliced into bars,
the great vats of boiling liquid
tended, day in, day out, for almost forty years.)

Shine for a dime!
He pitched the catchphrase high,
mimicking the shoe shine boys
whose cries he'd heard on the streets of Pittsburgh.
That's where he learned to smoke Havanas,
he confided, still puffing on a fat cigar;
and where he finally found his father,
propped up against a downtown bar.

Helena Rubenstein

Teetering on stiletto heels
she see-sawed to the bar to place her order.
A dry Martini with a teeny slice of lemon
and a packet of those cheesy biscuits
she intoned, her cut glass accent
honed through years of rubbing shoulders
with the nouveau-riche in Richards,
the high-class retail specialists
in ladies wear and evening dress,
where she was *almost manageress.*

Helena Rubenstein we called her,
smirking at her layers of rouge,
the ruby lipstick with handbag to match.
Scarlet nails peeled off
the cellophane from her cheesy snack
as she sang the praises
of Hardy Amies and Lachasse
or eulogised about her other half,
He's big in underwear you know,
hobnobs with all the gentry and top brass.

Her fifth Martini was the tipping point.
From then on she fell silent,
mouth set in a weary grin,
eyes fighting to focus on some far horizon.
The truth remained her secret
until after she passed on;
how, abandoned by three husbands,
she'd lived alone in a council flat
up seven flights of stairs,
and hadn't worked for years.

Coaly

The coal man came on crutches, wheezed his way to the bar
and flopped down on the bench seat in the corner.

His dark moustache twitched wildly with the effort, hands both
grabbing the table-edge, head thrown back to catch his breath.

There was no need to order. Dad always had his pint of bitter
at the ready, took it round and placed it by him, like a waiter.

Sticks propped against the wall, he grinned his thanks, his eyes
flashing brief reminders of a dust-filled past and happier days.

His voice was deep and rasping. Words came in bursts, heaving
their way between gasps and laboured, heavy breathing.

Conversation proved too hard for all but the few who sat down
close to him, prepared to invest their time. Most left him alone.

He fumbled in his pockets, struggled to extract a cigarette,
then held it in his teeth and forced a trembling match to light it,

aware it would make him cough, but persevering nevertheless,
his stooping, wasted frame not ready to relinquish this,

his final pleasure. He sat and smoked for hours, determined
to win a kind of victory just by being there. Refusing to give in.

Pat and Roland

Unusual couple. Chalk and cheese.
Four kids, three cats, a dog called Wanker,
several guinea pigs. No *please*
or *thank you* graced their lingua franca.

Moved to Kirkstall from Kirklees.
High-rise council block. Dim light,
damp walls. A broken lift. No trees.
They came out drinking every night.

Pat wore boots above her knees,
tight skirts, black leather, sixties stuff.
Loved clubbing and The Three Degrees.
Roland was an opera buff

whose god was Jussi Bjorling. *He's
the tops,* he'd say. *I've been a fan
for years.* Pat fiddled with her keys,
looked bored to tears, dreamed of the tan

she got in Torremolinos. *The sea's
so blue down there,* she'd sigh. *Seven
times we've been.* Roland would squeeze
her thigh. His idea of heaven

was listening to his old LPs,
The Desert Song and *Brigadoon.*
Hers was a sunbed, slow striptease,
Demis Roussos, Mills and Boon.

Rag and Bone

Rags 'n bones, rags 'n bones!
Bring out all your rags 'n bones!

On the dot of half past one he came,
flat cap pulled down over one eye,
five o'clock shadow dappling his face,
his horse clip-clopping
over cobbles in the yard.

He tethered her to a rusty hook
then staggered in, already unsteady
from stemming his thirst in other pubs
en route. He smelt of snuff, sawdust,
coughed a lot and rarely spoke.

His manner was always gruff,
except when he offered water
to his horse, his left hand
tenderly stroking her nose,
the right easing a bucket near her feet.

She nuzzled him before she drank,
the two of them lost
in a world of their own making,
somewhere silent, reverent,
beyond their understanding.

Bomber Harris

He talked of Lancasters, a bomber's moon,
his midnight raid on Dresden, navigating
only by the stars; of coming home
on a wing and a prayer, underbelly vibrating,
fuselage pockmarked with ack-ack fire; of how
he learned to fly in strict formation, turn
and dive through turbulent skies, swoop down low
on enemy targets, then head for the Channel at dawn.

He'd kept the moustache, his love of black and tan.
His wings and flying suit were traded for
a job in sales, a house with wife and son;
his compass for a road map, company car.
Now, every night, he drowned out salesman's patter
by reaching for the only life that mattered.

Mrs. Malaprop

I'll try an advocate with caribou
tonight, she said. *I feel a bit ambitious.*
Our Edie 'ad a pina colarado
at the bingo and, by, it was judicious!

Big and buxom, she was jolly without
her namesake's rudeness or pomposity.
Would do anyone a favour – *I'll 'elp*
you with the greatest animosity

she'd cry, clutching her capacious handbag
to her spacious breast. Lived with her sister
Edie, who was sickly, always in or
out of hospital. *She's under that Mister*

Sparrow in ornithology again.
'E says he's thinkin' about a replacement hip.
*I told 'im straight – just fix our **Edie's** pelmet.*
It 'asn't 'alf been giving 'er some gip.

She's been in there before you know, last year.
'Ad burial meals and tubes pushed down 'er throat.
They offered 'er seduction but she opted
to be numbed with local antidote.

The op went well and Mrs. M popped in
to celebrate. *I'm letting down my hair,*
she said. *They've finally given Ede some crotches*
and she's out of that offensive care!

Peggy and Hedley

That man's a nasty bit of work, gran said.
You mark my words, he's got a bit on the side,
a floozy. Never trust a man in suede.

My mother didn't agree. *Full of hot air*
but harmless was her view. I wasn't sure.
I watched him bending everybody's ear

except his wife's. He barely noticed her.
She smiled, edged back slowly in her chair
and shrank into the grey fur of her collar.

Every half an hour he'd insist
on buying a round. *Reckon if wifey's sloshed*
I might have fun tonight, you get my gist?

Sometimes, Peggy spoke to others round
her table but always sounded anxious. *It rained*
a lot last night, she'd say, wringing her hands,

but then it often does in March. Her laugh
was high-pitched, nervous, followed by a cough.
As soon as Hedley thought she'd said enough

he gagged her with a glance, all the while
fixing his mouth in a grin he thought would fool
his friends, convince them he was listening still.

One closing time, she stood beside the fire,
her face reflected in a nearby mirror.
There, in her eyes, I caught a glimpse of terror.

The Regular

We set our watches by him. On the stroke
of eight he came in every night for years,
returning from a job he rarely spoke
much of, to do with people in arrears.

He leaned against the bar, reserved, withdrawn
but never rude. His speech was soft, laconic,
delivered with a smile; his humour, born
of insight, always clever and ironic.

Lost in reverie like some ancient scholar,
he'd take his Guinness and then hesitate,
gazing at contours in its creamy collar
as if, like tea leaves, they could tell his fate.

The details of his personal life were vague,
devoid of any colour, like his clothes.
He had a wife, a teenage son called Craig,
the rest he was reluctant to disclose.

He drank for hours, motionless, at ease
with near unconsciousness, remained unseen
till, roused by cries of *Time! Last orders please!*
he'd take his pint and play the fruit machine.

That Friday he struck lucky. We heard the clatter
as chaotic jackpot coins belched free
above the froth and buzz of late night chatter
and drunken voices singing out of key.

He filled his hands with silver, scraped the pile
inside a plastic bag that someone gave.
He left with just the flicker of a smile,
his customary farewell nod and wave.

Next day they found him (no sign of a note)
stretched out behind a disused railway shed;
the windfall coins now weighing down his coat,
the windfall plastic bag around his head.

Closing Time: Christmas 1965

We watch the dark italics start to flicker
on the starched white linen tablecloth
and huddle round the whirr of the projector.
The first film with my brand new cine camera . . .

Licking his lips beside the cooker,
dad lifts aloft what's left of the turkey
while mam adopts that wooden posture
she reserves for every picture.

There's a fleeting glimpse of a distant corner
where grandma's quietly nodding off
still overcome by Christmas dinner
and then we're into the closing-time clamour.

Unaware the lens is on her,
my mother hunts for empty pints,
slotting one inside the other
as deftly as a conjuror.

Hordes of customers surge behind her,
desperate for a final tipple.
They push and scrabble to place an order,
some waving hands, one waving a fiver.

Now grandma's awake and wiping the counter
in her pinny, a flimsy yellow
paper hat from a Christmas cracker
still clinging to the back of her

and Drunken Derek's terrier
is stretched full length beside the fire.
She opens one eye to check her master
hasn't gone to meet his maker . . .

Everything stops as abruptly as it began.
No fanfares or codas, no list of crew or cast,
no time to adjust as the empty spool spins on.
All of us are there and then . . . we're gone.

Indigo Dreams Publishing Ltd
24, Forest Houses
Cookworthy Moor
Halwill
Beaworthy
Devon
EX21 5UU
www.indigodreams.co